ANCIENT IRISH AIRS AND DANCES

201 Classic Tunes Arranged for Piano

Collected and Edited by
GEORGE PETRIE

Arranged for Piano by
F. HOFFMANN

DOVER PUBLICATIONS, INC.
Mineola, New York

Published in the United Kingdom by David & Charles, Brunel House, Forde Close, Newton Abbot, Devon TQ12 4PU.

Bibliographical Note

This Dover edition, first published in 2002, is an unabridged republication of *Ancient Music of Ireland from the Petrie Collection, Arranged for the Pianoforte by F. Hoffmann,* originally published by Pigott & Co., Dublin, 1877.
A footnoote in the original indicated that the Dirge on p. 133 was reprinted from William Beauford's paper on Ancient Irish Lamentations, 1791.

International Standard Book Number: 0-486-42426-X

Manufactured in the United States of America
Dover Publications, Inc., 31 East 2nd Street, Mineola, N.Y. 11501

CONTENTS

TO

WILLIAM STOKES, M.D.,

D.C.L., F.R.S.

SIR,

The most grateful tribute I can offer to Dr. Petrie's memory is to associate with those Airs he loved so well the name of his dearest and most valued friend ; allow me, therefore, to inscribe to you this Volume of the Petrie Collection, and to remain,

With sincere respect,

Your faithful Servant,

F. HOFFMANN.

ANCIENT MUSIC OF IRELAND.

1

The Sigh.

The Roving Pedlar.

The Yellow Garron.
(An Gearran Buidh.)

poco piu animato

rall.

dim.

p

4

Air.
(Name Unknown.)

♩ = 60.

Andante
Affettuoso.

p

p

p

mf

p

pp

dolente

pp

rit.

pp

5

Little Donnell.

(Domnal Og.)

♩ = 66.

Moderato.

p cantabile.

6

Air.

(Name Unknown.)

♩ = 80.

Allegro non Troppo.

Air.
(Name Unknown.)

6

8

Where were you all Day my pretty Boy.

9

Sligo Lullaby.

O my Girl along with me.

(O mo chaillin le mise.)

Far beyond yon Mountain.

Air.

(Name Unknown.)

12

13

Gramachree, but I love you well.

14

The Strolling Mason.

15

The Maiden Ray.

16

Hop Jig.

Oh! shrive me Father.

18

Air.
(Name Unknown.)

Stately Sarah.

I'm a poor Stranger.

The Yellow Sand.

(Gainibh buidh.)

22
Oh what shall I do with this silly old Man.

There is a lone House.

24

Carolan's Lament for Charles Maccabe.

♩ = 96.
Lento
con
Malinconia.

The Ewe with the crooked Horn.

My Wife is sick.

27

The Kerry Boys.

Awhile as thou wert.

(Tamal da rabhsai.)

29

Cradle Song.

30

A Lament.

31

Arthur of this Town.

Rose with the snowy Skin and raven Hair.

(Rois geal dubh.)

33

The Deserter.

34

The Banks of Ahasnagh.

35

I will raise my Sail.

36

Emigrant Song.

37

The Lobster Pot.

38

Mayo Air.
(Name Unknown.)

39

I will never deceive you.

The moving Bog.

Black eyed Susan.

42

Air.
(Name Unknown.)

43

Arran Air.

44

Better let them alone.

45

I'm lost without her.

Alas! O, thou World's Gem.

(Uch, on a chuid don ts-aeguil.)

Air.

(Name Unknown.)

48

O, Mary thy Laugh is sweet.

(O, Maire is deas do gaire.)

Planxty Drew.

Nurse's Tune.

52

Beside the River Loune.

53

Curly Locks.

54

Red Regan and the Nun.

55

The Gaol of Clonmell.

56

The Pearl of the fair poll of Hair.

A Lament.

58

Limerick Air.

59

The cutting of the Hay.

60

In Miltown I heard the music.

The Soldier's Song.

62

The Sails were unfurled.

Ancient Clan March.

64

I wish, I wish, but I wish in vain.

My Love he is tall although he is young.

Luinneach—from Ossians Poems.

Munster Jig.

The Banks of the Daisies.

69
Molly Asthore.

70
Air.
(Name Unknown.)

71

The Pearl of the Yellow Road.

72

Rossaviel.

73

Luggelaw.

74
Air.
(Name Unknown.)

50

Air.

(Name Unknown.)

76

Handsome Molly Nugent.

(Molli breagh Nugent.)

77
Spinning Song.

78

Open the door Love.

79

Arranmore Boat Song.

Cathleen.

81
Clare Reel.

84

A Caoine.

The Great Mountain.
(Sliab Mor.)

Lullaby.

Johnny Cox.

Ree Raw.

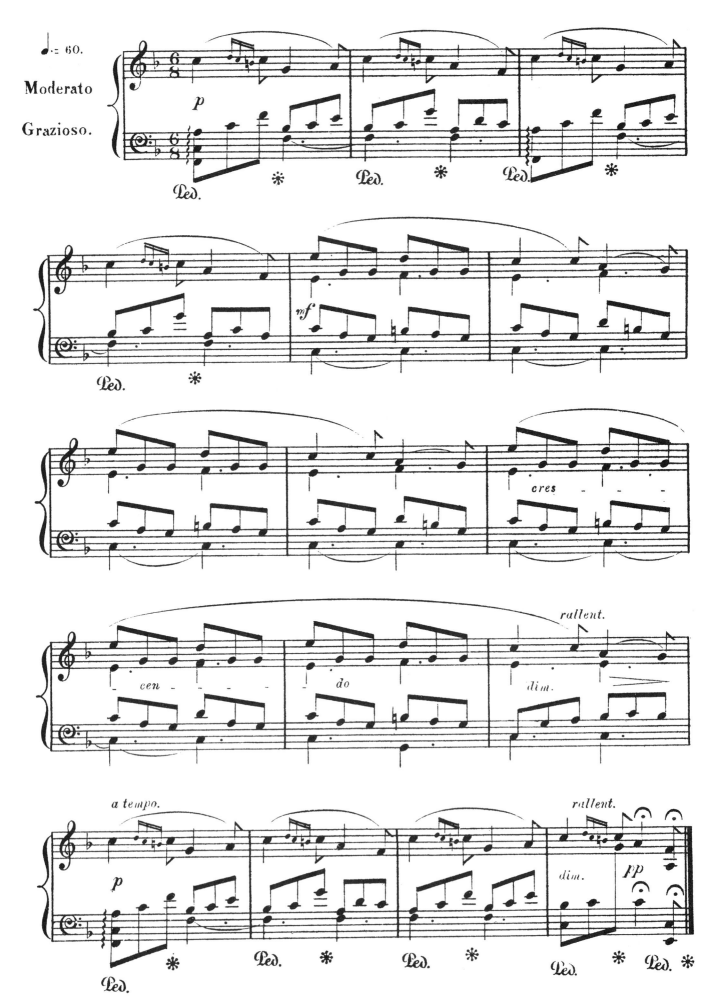

Air.
(Name Unknown.)

Lento.

90

A Song of Castle Hacket.

Allegretto con Tenerezza.

91

A Cork Reel.

Patrick Sarsfield.

Molly my Jewel.

94

Lament for Una Mac Dermot.

♪=80.

Adagio
con
Duolo.

Il basso marcato.

95

Coady's Dream.

♩=100.

Allegro
Grazioso.

96

Biddy I'm not jesting.

Sheela my Love.

98
I'm a young little Girl.
(Is cailin beg go me.)

99
Air.
(Name Unknown.)

100

The crooked old Man.

(Ar seanduine crom.)

101

Donnell O'Daly.

102

Ballyvaughan.

O Mary Asthore.

104
Air.
(Name Unknown.)

Far far down in the South of Luidach.

Oh fair John my Love.

107

Planxty.

Last Night I dreamt of my own true Love.

My hearts Love is He.

He knew you not.

I'd roam the World over with you.

74

The hornless Cow.

I'm a Rover.

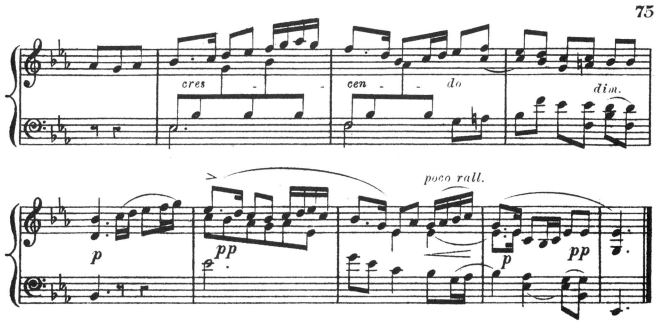

114

The Eagles Whistle.

Arranmore Tune.

116

March Tune.

117

Air.
(Name Unknown.)

118

Beautiful Molly McKeon.

119

About the Cauldron.

120

Song of the Ghost.

121

Cradle Song.

122

A Reel.

123

An Erris Melody.

82

124

Air.

(Name Unknown)

125

The Maids of Mourne Shore.

126

Black Burke.

127

Hag, you've killed me.

128

Farewell.

129
Air.
(Name Unknown.)

130

I shall leave this Country.

131

Jig.

132

The good Ship Planet.

133

The old Coolin.

134

A little before Day.

135

With her Dog and her Gun.

136

A Cork Reel.

137

My Woe and my Loss.

(Mo chreach is mo dhith.)

138

The Irish Lad's a Jolly Boy.

139

Air.

(Name Unknown.)

140

Jig.

141

Knockreany.

142

Welcome, thy Health.

(Dia bheatha do slainte.)

143

One Night I dreamed.

144

When she answered me her Voice was low.

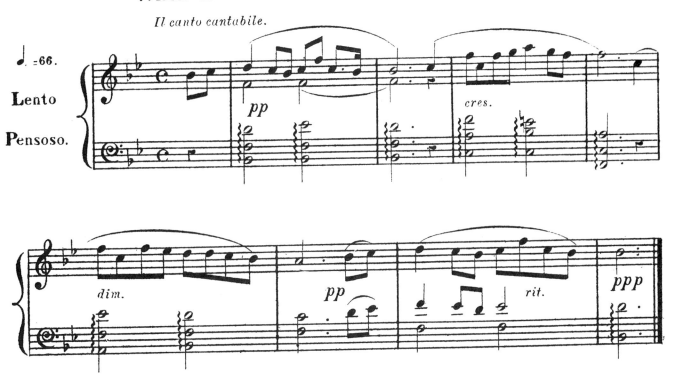

The little red Lark.

A Woman's Lament for the Death of her Hen.

147
Jig.

Presto
con
Spirito.

148

Air.

(Name Unknown.)

149

Dear Eileen I'm going to leave you.

150

Yesterday Morning and I about to sleep.

151

My Love, what is the reason you cannot fancy me.

152

The Lament of Wm Mc Peter.

153
Lovely Nancy.

¹⁵⁴

Reel.

¹⁵⁵

Connemara Air.

156

Air.

(Name Unknown.)

Allegro
Risoluto.

104

Come sit down beside me, my own Heart's Delight.

Air.
(Name Unknown.)

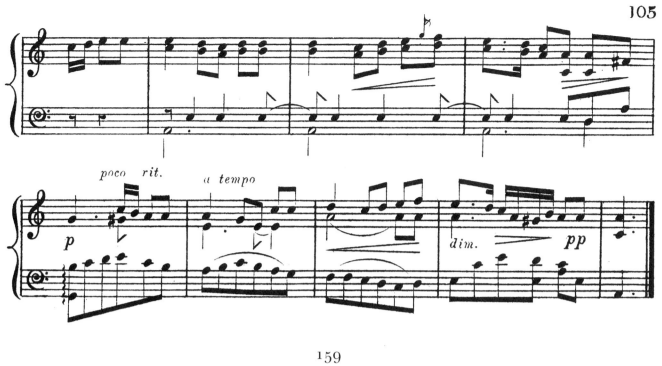

159

The brave Irish Lad.

162

Air.

(Name Unknown.)

Molto cantabile ed espressivo.

Allegretto Grazioso.

163

Her Skin is like the Lily.

164

The stout little Boy.

Buachailín havel.

If I'm alive in Ireland.

Adieu my lovely Peggy.

167

Cahan O'Hara.

168

Air.

(Name Unknown.)

Andante Cantabile.

♪ = 108.

169

Priests over the Border.

(Sagairt tar teorach.)

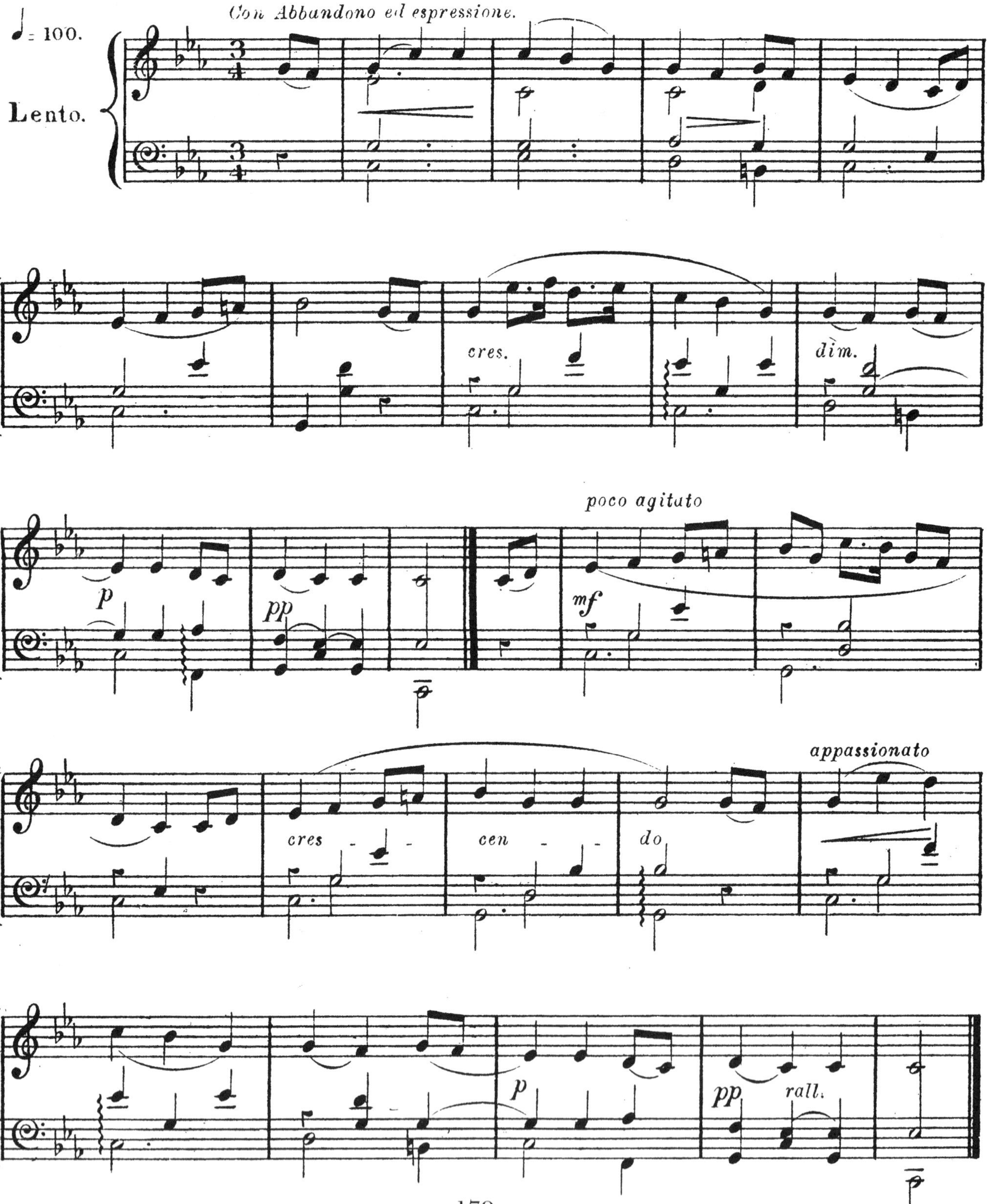

Con Abbandono ed espressione.
♩ = 100.
Lento.
cres.
dim.
p
pp
poco agitato
mf
cres - cen - do
appassionato
p
pp
rall.

170

Air.

(Name Unknown.)

♩. = 84.
Allegretto
Scherzando.

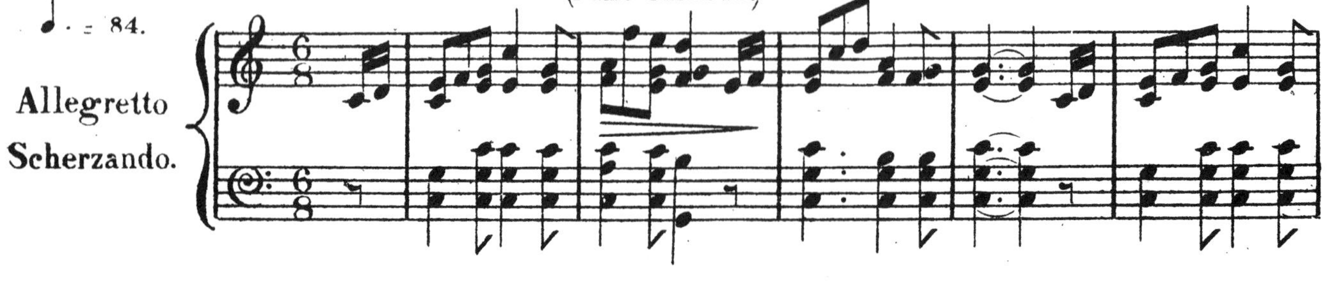

171

The Four Seasons.

172

Cradle Song.

172

Sligo Air.

174
Arranmore Air.

Lady Gordon's Minuet.

Air.

(Name Unknown.)

If I and my true Love.

(Da mbeinnse ogus mo ghradh ban.)

178

Spinning Song.

179

The winnowing Sheet

(An Caitech Roin.)

180
Air.
(Name Unknown.)

Bessie of Dromore.

O Whisky my dear.

(A fhuisce a mhuirnin.)

Allegretto Innocente. ♩ = 66.

p e legato

p *pp*

Air.

(Name Unknown.)

Moderato. ♩ = 120.

mf *p*

cres. *dim.*

p *pp*

The Lovers Complaint.

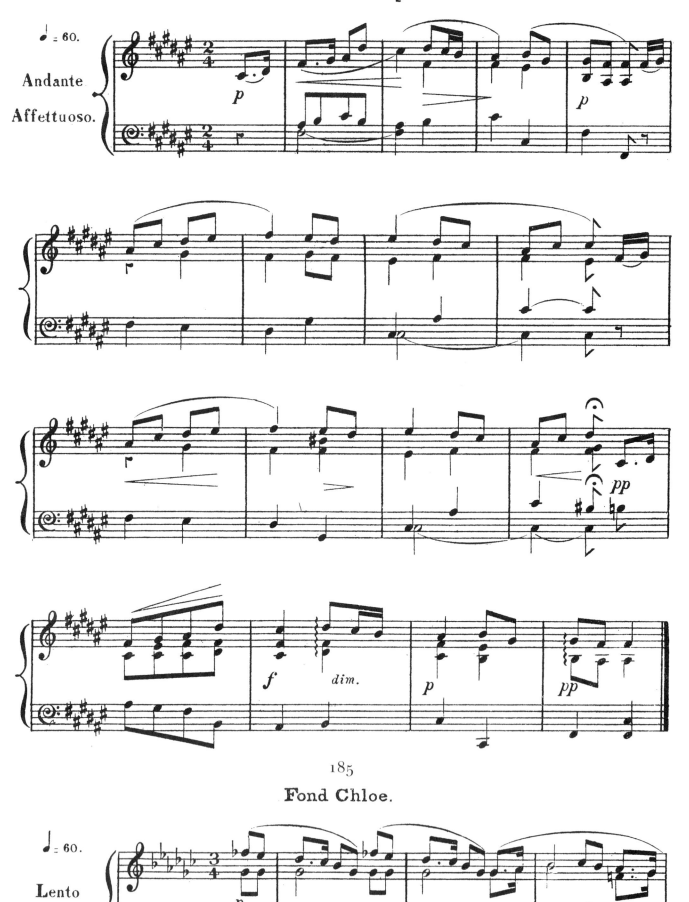

184

Fond Chloe.

186

In the beginning of the Summer.

(A dtv.is ant samhra.)

Mor of Cloyne.

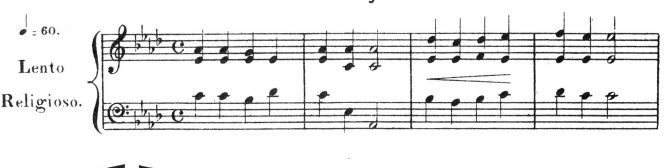

I lost my Love.

191

Ancient Caoine.

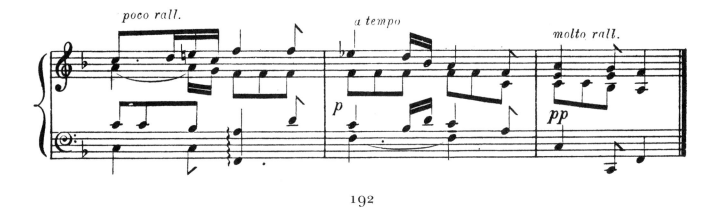

192

Savourneen Deelish.

¹⁹³
A Plaint.

Song of the Woods.

¹⁹⁵

I'll make my Love a Breast of Glass.

196

Scorching is this Love.

SPECIMENS OF THE ANCIENT

CHURCH MUSIC OF IRELAND.

Chant.

Hymn.

Hymn.

Hymn.

Hymn.

(From Ossians Poems.)

Caoinan or Dirge.

Largo

Solenne.

sotto voce.

First Semi-Chorus.

Alla

Recitativo.

Second Semi-Chorus.

Alla

Recitativo.

Full Chorus.

Tempo

Perduto.

Lento

Funerale.

First Semi-Chorus.

Recitativo

Parlante.

Second Semi-Chorus.

Recitativo

Parlante.

Full Chorus.

Moderato.

The following three Airs are from Queen Elizabeth's Virginal Book. They have been already published by Mr W. Chappell in his Work on "Popular Music of the olden Time," Vol. II. page 793, and are reprinted here by that Author's kind permission.

The Irish Ho-Hoane.
(Ochone.)

The Irish Dumpe.

Callino Casturame.

Moderato Semplice.

It is evidently to this tune that Shakespeare alludes in the play of Henry the Fifth, Act IV. Sc. 4. where Pis_ tol on meeting a French soldier, exclaims "Quality! Calen o custure me." In the folio we find "Calmie custure me," which has been turned, in the modern Editions, into "Call you me?_ Construe me," Malone found among "Sundry new Sonets in a handefull of pleasant Delites 1584," a Sonet of a lover in praise of his Lady to "Calen o custure me," sung at every line's end. In M! Lovers "Lyrics of Ireland," he notices the resemblance of the first word to the name "Caillino," speaking of M!s Fitzsimon's beautiful Poem, "The Woods of Caillino," and adds_ M! Boswell, in his Edition of Shakespeare says that M! Finnegan, Master of the school established in London for the education of the Irish, says the words mean "Little Girl of my Heart for ever and ever," now this is not the meaning, and I can_ not but wonder that, with so much literary discussion as has taken place on the subject, the true spelling, and conse_ quently, the meaning of the burden have remained till now undiscovered. The burden, as given in the "Handefull of plea_ sant Delites," and copied by Malone, is "Calen o custure me" which is an attempt to spell, and pretty nearly represents the sound of "Colleen oge astore," and those words mean "Young Girl, my Treasure." Stokes's life of **Petrie, p. 431.**